3 COMING TO
THE CHURCH

SADLIER'S
New Edition
Coming to Faith Program

Activity Book

William H. Sadlier, Inc.
9 Pine Street
New York, New York 10005-1002

TABLE OF CONTENTS

Unit 3 Our Church and Our Parish

Unit 4 United in Our Catholic Church

Dear Family,

Last year your child learned about the celebration of the Eucharist, our great memorial of Jesus' loving sacrifice for us, and the celebration of God's forgiveness in the sacrament of Reconciliation.

This year your child continues the journey in faith with you. At this age your child is still a participant in your faith. This will continue to be true until your child achieves the mature, personal faith we hope for them. This year your child explores the life of the Church, not only the universal Church, but the Church as it touches your family most, in your parish. This year opens your child ever more to an assembly, a community of faithful people who gather, celebrate, proclaim the message, and carry on the mission to bringing about the presence or kingdom of God in this time and in this place.

Throughout this year your child will learn anew, and you will be invited to remember anew, too. Seize this opportunity to learn again, to see through the eyes of a child the mission of the Church. Take this opportunity to reflect on the enduring structures, events, and celebrations that nourish and support us all. Recall again that the Church is one, holy, catholic, and apostolic.

See anew how your role and your child's role are vital to the growth of the Kingdom today. When your family is present, the Church is enriched. This is as true today as it was in first century Palestine and Greece and Rome.

The activities presented in these pages are for you to use and adapt to fit your family. Let them be a joyous part of the ebb and flow of your family's unique brand of order and chaos! Try to make these activities and prayers part of your busy days, and as a family enjoy the challenge of Coming to the Church.

Sincerely,

The Sadlier Family

Parish, Family, and Me

Dear Family,
In this lesson your child learned that the Church is a gathering of the friends and followers of Jesus. These activities help bring that message home.

My Parish Is a Community of Friends

Write the name of someone in your parish who is a friend and disciple of Jesus.

prays with me.

shows me how to serve.

teaches me about God.

loves me.

Our Parish

Whether our parish is large or small,
We are all for one and one for all.

In our prayer and work and play,
We try to follow in Jesus' way.

Wherever we go, our paths are blest.
Whatever we do, we give our best.

Look in your parish bulletin. Write down something your parish community does to show that your parish is a community of Jesus' friends.

_____

_____

_____

_____

_____

_____

Think about ways your family can be part of the parish's loving service to others.

Reconciliation

Dear Family,
In this lesson your child reviewed Reconciliation and celebrated a service of forgiveness. This activity will help your child review the celebration of Reconciliation.

These are the steps in celebrating Reconciliation. Read these and briefly explain what you know about each one.

1. We remember—examination of conscience

2. We tell God we are sorry—Act of Contrition

3. We tell our sins to the priest—confession

4. The priest says words of forgiveness—absolution

5. We say or do something to show we will try to do better—penance

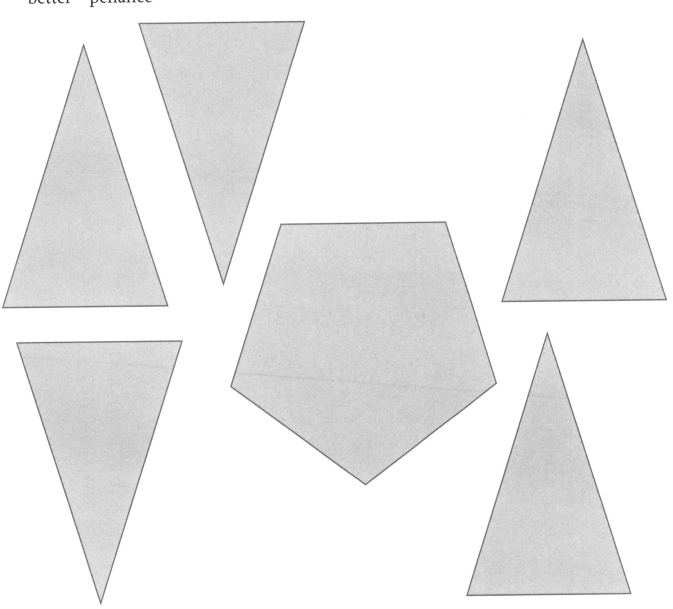

Now turn the page over to make a star that shows you know how to celebrate the Sacrament of Reconciliation.

Cut out the shape that has 5 sides. Cut out the triangles. Put the triangles in order around the shape. Paste the triangles and the shape on another piece of paper. Cut out the star and mount it as a reminder.

Eucharist

Dear Family,
In this lesson your child prepared for and celebrated the Eucharist. Use these activity pages to help your family make Sunday special.

Table Blessing

Here is a prayer to pray with your family at a meal.

† **All:** In the name of the Father and of the Son and of the Holy Spirit. Amen.

Leader: As we gather to celebrate, we remember Jesus' love for us.

All: The Lord is with us always.

Leader: As we offer thanks for our family and friends, we remember all God's gifts.

All: The Lord is with us always.

✂

Leader: As we give thanks for this food,
 we remember the poor and hungry.
All: The Lord is with us always.
Leader: When we forgive and ask forgiveness,
 we remember God's mercy and love.
All: The Lord is with us always.
Leader: Before we share this meal in friendship
 and love, let us pray as Jesus taught us:
All: Our Father . . .

Directions: Use this strip as a pattern on another piece of paper to make one for each table guest. Cut out the circles along the dashed lines. Paste the circles on the strips. Put the strips around the napkins and secure them.

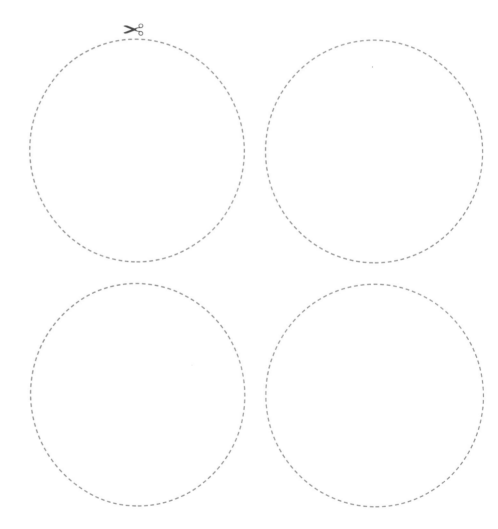

Our Parish Prays

Learning to Pray

It is not always easy to pray. Jesus knew that sometimes we don't "feel" like praying.

But Jesus wanted us to know that prayer is much more than feelings. We can pray whether our hearts are full or empty. That is why Jesus taught His friends to pray. We must learn to pray better, too.

Who teaches you to pray?

_____

_____

With whom do you like to pray?

_____

_____

Dear Family,
In this lesson your child learned that prayer is talking and listening to God and that we can call on the saints to pray with and for us. Use this activity to help your child become a better parish pray-er.

Turn the page to find a way to be the best pray-er you can be.

Be the Best Pray-er You Can Be

How can you be the best pray-er you can be? What are the best ways for you to pray? In each list below, circle the one thing that you think will best help you become a better pray-er. Then write out the kind of pray-er you want to be.

Prayer Place
my bedroom
outdoors
church
kitchen
living room
other

_____

Prayer Time
when I wake up
before meals
before bedtime
after school
late morning
other

_____

Prayer Position
sitting
standing
walking
kneeling
other

_____

Prayer Help
the Bible
a crucifix
music
a statue
other

_____

Prayer Starters
praying with my own words
quieting myself
saying a favorite prayer
thinking about the saints
other

_____

Prayer Partners
classmates
family members
Sunday assembly
friends
other

_____

This is the kind of pray-er I want to be.

_____

_____

_____

_____

Our Parish Worships

Dear Family,
This lesson introduced your child to the seven sacraments of the Church, which are signs of God's love and care for us in Christ. As you share this activity, point out the many ways your child can be a sign of God's loving care to others.

Signs of Something More

Look at the welcome mat, snowflake, and animal tracks pictured on this page. Each is a *sign* of something more. Each points to something else—something important. In the frame under each sign, draw what you think each might be a sign of.

  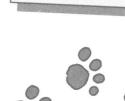

Might be a sign of . . .   Might be a sign of . . .   Might be a sign of . . .

Signs of Loving Care

The sacraments are powerful signs of God's love and care for us. The sacraments help us become signs of God's love for others.

Read these three small stories. Pick one and draw or write an ending that shows how you could be a sign of God's love and care.

Old Mr. Bren is sick. His family lives far away. No one ever visits him. He is lonely and sad.

Twan is new to your school. She has no friends and feels lost. She wishes she could belong.

Your parish has a homeless shelter. Families with little children come there. Your parish needs someone to play with these children.

Dear Family,
In this lesson your child explored the sacrament of Reconciliation and discovered how we celebrate it as a parish. Use this activity to "ground" your parish celebration in your home.

Planning Family Reconciliation

You know how we celebrate reconciliation as a parish. Now you can plan how to celebrate reconciliation at home.

1. Choose a **story of reconciliation** from the Bible. If you wish, share one of the following stories:

   Luke 15:4–7   Luke 15:8–10

   Matthew 18:21–22

2. Decide how to **present the story:** One reader? More than one? Acting it out?

3. Write a family **prayer of sorrow** for selfishness and sin. Start your prayer with these words:

   † **Forgiving God, we are sorry for . . .**

   _____

   _____

4. Agree on a family **promise of reconciliation** to help you be more caring and forgiving toward others. Write what you decide here.

   _____

   _____

5. Write a family **prayer of praise** to give thanks to God for reconciling you to one another.

   † **Loving God, we give You praise for . . .**

   _____

   _____

6. Finally, choose a family member to be the "Leader" in your celebration.

Turn the page to celebrate reconciliation with your family.

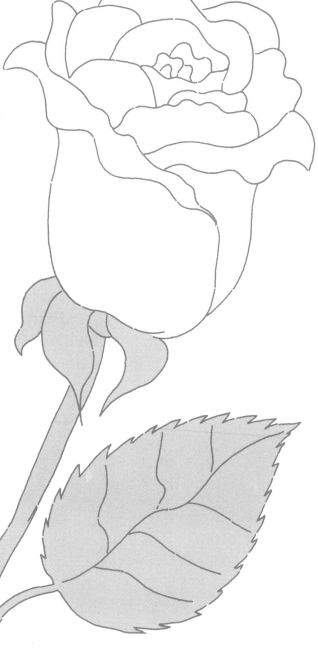

Celebrating Family Reconciliation

Gathering

Leader: Let us call on God for forgiveness and reconciliation.

All: Open us, Lord, to receive Your reconciling love. Open us, Lord, to hear Your Word of love.

The Word of God

(Present the Bible story of reconciliation you chose.)

Prayer of Sorrow

(Pray your family prayer of sorrow.)

Promise of Reconciliation

Leader: Let us proclaim our promise of reconciliation together.

(Read the family promise you agreed on.)

Prayer of Praise

All: Pray your family prayer of praise.)

After your celebration, make a family reconciliation banner. From construction paper, cut out a pennant shape. Write, *"We are reconcilers who . . ."* Then add words of forgiveness you can say and acts of forgiveness you can do. Decorate your banner and post it in your home.

Our Church and the Bible

Family Stories

You are a member of a family. Your family has many stories. Think of a family story that is important to you. What is the story about? Who told you the story? What special message does the story tell about your family? Write your favorite family story here. Be sure to share the story with others in your family.

My Family's Stories

Bible Reading Chart

We are members of God's family. The Bible is filled with stories about God's love for us. The Bible is our storybook. Use this chart with your family Bible to discover and share some of the wonderful stories of God. They are our stories, too!

Reader's Name	Bible Story	Book of the Bible	Message

Our Church as a Community

Community Calls

People in a community help and serve one another. Community people come when they are called. Tell who you would call if . . .

A house is on fire.

A child is lost.

Someone gets sick.

Someone wishes to be baptized.

You feel afraid.

Explain how each person you called would serve and help.

Dear Family,
In this lesson your child learned that each of us has a vocation to serve God and our Church in a special way. Use this activity to help your child recognize that he or she can begin to live out this vocation now.

God Calls

You have a vocation. "Vocation" means an invitation or **call** to help and serve. God called you when you were baptized. Every day God's call to you will become clearer. As you grow, you will discover your own special vocation. But you can help and serve right now, too.

Read these short stories. Choose one and decide how you could answer the call to help and serve. Draw what you would do.

Someone in your school is lonely and has no one to play with. How could you help and serve?

New neighbors have no parish to belong to. How could you help and serve?

Some people in your community have no homes and are hungry. How could you help and serve?

Our Church and the Kingdom

Dear Family,
In this lesson your child discovered that the kingdom of God is the power of God's life and love in the world. Use this activity to help your child appreciate that he or she can be a sign of God's love.

Good Soil

Look at this picture and pretend you are a farmer. Finish drawing the picture, showing a place where you could grow a plant. Mark an "X" where your seed would go. Then draw a picture of your plant full grown.

The kingdom, or reign, of God is planted in the very best of places. Do you know where that is? Finish this rhyme to find out.

> Way deep down inside us,
> Is where God's kingdom starts.
> Thank You, God, for planting
> Your reign within our ___ ___ ___ ___ ___ .

Turn the page to see how God's Kingdom grows.

Building Up God's Kingdom

People who help build up the kingdom of God live s' Law of Love. They are just and fair. ey are peacemakers. Draw a circle around he "Kingdom people" you see. Tell wh u think they are signs of God's Kingdo n the world.

4

Easter

SIGNS OF EASTER

The Easter Moon

Did you know that Easter does not happen on the same Sunday every year? That is because Easter is celebrated on the first Sunday following the first full moon after the first day of Spring. Check a calendar to find out when the springtime full moon will shine. Then, gather with your family to view the full moon that sets the date for this year's celebration of Easter.

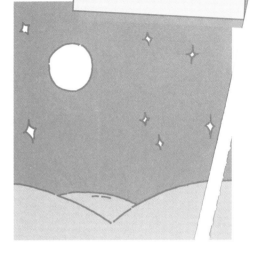

Easter Eggs

Eggs have long been signs of springtime and new life. Many years ago eating eggs was forbidden during Lent, so on Easter Sunday people would give one another gifts of decorated eggs. These "Easter eggs" then became signs of the tomb out of which Christ gloriously rose to new life. We have a special blessing for Easter eggs. After you color your eggs, use this blessing:

† O Lord, bless these eggs. Make them a healthy food for your faithful people, who will gratefully share them in honor of the resurrection of our Lord Jesus Christ. Amen.

Easter Grass

A wonderful springtime sign of new life is the grass that is beginning to sprout. You can grow some very special Easter grass. A week or two before Easter, put soil in a container. Spread grass seed. Keep the seed watered, but in a dark place. Don't worry. The grass will grow, but it will be a different color, an Easter color. Try it and see.

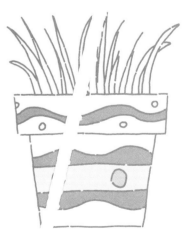

Turn the page to learn new ways to celebrate Easter.

Easter Blessings

Count your blessings. With your family, make a list of the many ways God has blessed you. Use the list in your family's Easter prayers of thanks and praise. Start your list here:

_____

_____

_____

_____

_____

Easter Alleluia

Do you remember the "Signs of Lent" box you made at the beginning of Lent? Now is the time to open it up. Have an adult help you cut it apart and turn it into an "Alleluia Cross" of Easter joy. Hang your "Alleluia Cross." Light a candle to remind you of Jesus Christ, the Light of the World. Then join with your family in this Easter prayer:

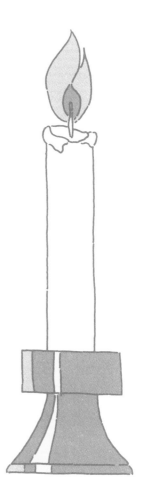

† Alleluia!
O God,
You bring us joy,
You give us new hearts,
You lift our spirits
in Jesus Christ our Lord.
Thank You for Your many blessings to us, especially . . .
    (Name some of the blessings you listed.)
Make us one people—Your Easter people.
Make us signs of joy and new life for all the world.
Amen.

The Church Is One and Holy

Dear Family,
In this lesson your child learned that the Church is one and holy. The activity on these pages will help your family see themselves as part of this one and holy Church.

Be **one** in Spirit, gathered in **one** hope, **one** Lord, **one** faith, **one** baptism, with **one** God and Father who is over all. Live as people called by God.

from Ephesians 4:1, 4–5

Cut out the circle. Cut a line from the edge to the dot. Paste the circle to make a shallow cone. Cut out each heart. Paste a photo of a family member or a friend on each heart. Attach each heart to the cone with a needle and thread.

PASTE

The Church is one. The Church is holy.

We Are All God's People

Use gestures to help you pray this Navajo prayer as a family.

Decorate this page.

Dear Family,
In this lesson your child learned to respect all who seek God in their work and prayer. These activity pages help reinforce that appreciation.

NAVAJO PRAYER

1. The world before me is renewed in beauty.

2. The world behind me is renewed in beauty.

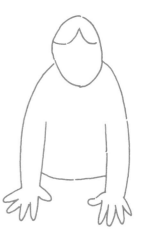

3. The world below me is renewed in beauty.

The world above me is renewed in beauty.

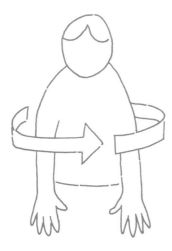

5. All things around me are renewed in beauty.

6. It is finished in beauty. It is finished in beauty. It is finished in beauty.

Mother Teresa of Calcutta works among the people of India. She asks us to do good work, too. She asks us to do something beautiful for God. Draw a picture of yourself doing something beautiful for God.

SOMETHING BEAUTIFUL FOR GOD

With love from _____

Mary, Mother of the Church

Joy in Mary's Life

1. The mystery of the Annunciation
   tells the coming of our salvation.

2. When Mary visited Elizabeth her cousin,
   Mary was called blessed among all women.

3. A sky full of angels sang, "Peace on earth,"
   on the wonderful night of Jesus' birth.

4. Joseph and Mary came to the Temple with joy,
   To present to God their little boy.

5. Once Jesus was lost, then He was found,
   in the Temple with teachers all around.

Turn the page to read the end of this rhyme.

55

From long ago as everyone knows,
The symbol of joy has been the rose.

All of Mary's joys strung together you see,
Have given us the name *Rosary*.

Directions. See page 55. Match the numbers next
to each event in Jesus' and Mary's life with the
joyful mysteries of the Rosary. Write the numbers
in the boxes.

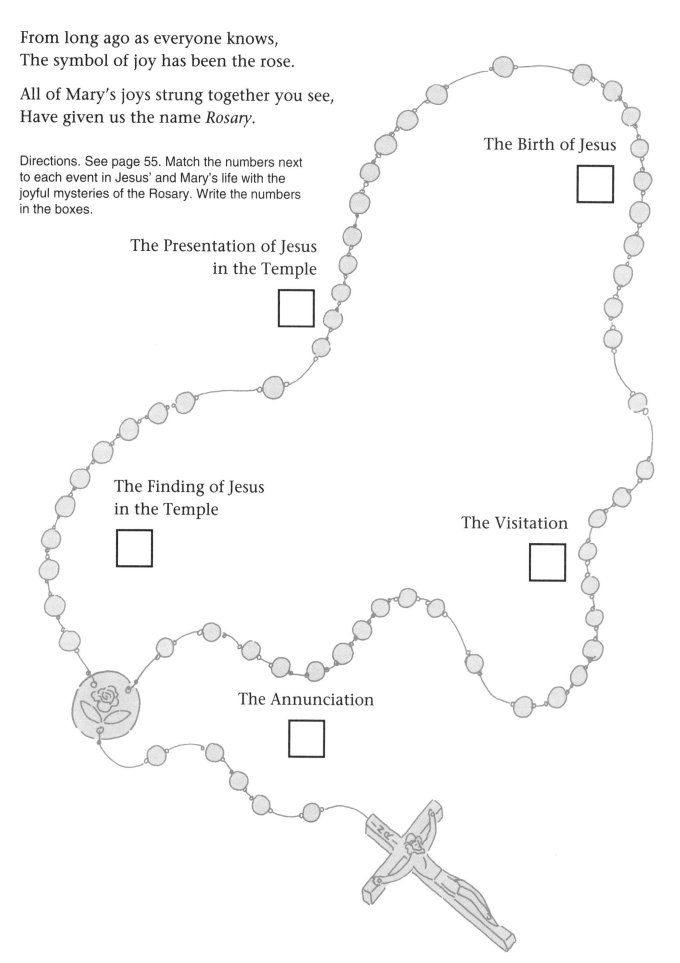

The Birth of Jesus

The Presentation of Jesus
in the Temple

The Finding of Jesus
in the Temple

The Visitation

The Annunciation

We Are the Church

The Juggler of Our Lady

Once upon a time, a legend says, a juggler joined a group of holy monks. The juggler saw all the wonderful things they did. He saw the baker monk bring his beautiful bread to Mary's altar. He saw the candle maker monk offer his bright candles. He saw the pictures the artist monk drew and the bright flowers of the gardener monk.

One night, the juggler stole down to the chapel to offer his gift. He threw one ball into the air, and then another ball, and another. The balls rose and fell in a bright pattern. He performed his tricks all night long. He grew so weary he fell asleep right at the feet of Mary.

As the sun peeked over the hills, the monk who rang the morning bell peeped into the chapel in time to see Mary bend down and bless the sleeping juggler.

We know this much is true:
When we give our best,
God in heaven sees
and our own gift is blest.

Think about the best gift you can give. Tell how you will use your gift for God.

_____

_____

_____

_____

_____

_____

_____

Prayer

Prayer Ways

Invite everyone in your family to choose a different color crayon. Have each family member select one dot in each column and connect them with one continuous line to discover his or her best way to pray.

Dear Family,
In this session your child discovered some of the many ways one can pray. These pages will help your family grow in prayer.

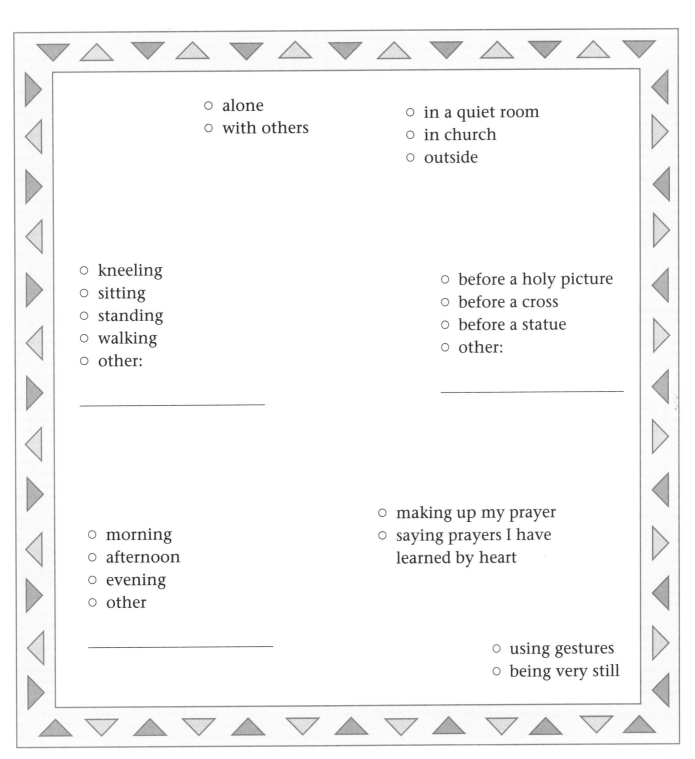

○ alone
○ with others

○ in a quiet room
○ in church
○ outside

○ kneeling
○ sitting
○ standing
○ walking
○ other:

_____

○ before a holy picture
○ before a cross
○ before a statue
○ other:

_____

○ morning
○ afternoon
○ evening
○ other

_____

○ making up my prayer
○ saying prayers I have
  learned by heart

○ using gestures
○ being very still

Decorate this page.

A Family Prayer for Evening

† O God, be our support all the day long
  until the shadows lengthen,
  and evening comes
  and the busy world is hushed,
  and our work is done.
  Then in Your mercy,
  grant us a safe lodging,
  and a holy rest,
  and peace at the last.
  Amen.

The Saints

Well done, good and faithful saints.
Enter into the joy of the Lord.

Connect the dots in numerical order. Then turn
over the page to learn about these saints.

Dear Family,
In this lesson your child learned that saints can be our heroes and models. Help your child with the activities on these two pages.

1. Andrew
2. Elizabeth Ann Seton
3. Francis of Assisi
4. Joseph
5. Kateri
6. Martin
7. Mary
8. Nicholas
9. Peter
10. Thérèse

Decorate this page and hang it up to remember
the saints.

Use the names of the saints on page 61.
Write the name of the saint after each clue.
The clues are in numerical order, too.

1. A fisherman and an apostle

   _____

2. A teacher, mother, and sister

   _____

3. He loved the beauty of God's world.

   _____

4. Mary's husband and guardian of Jesus

   _____

5. Member of the Iroquois people

   _____

6. A brother who helped the poor.

   _____

7. Mother of Jesus

   _____

8. He gave to others with love.

   _____

9. First leader of the whole Church

   _____

10. A patron saint of missionaries

   _____

Growing Together

Use your crayons to decorate this page.
Then turn to page 64.

Then turn to page 64.

Dear Family,
This prayer service asks God to bless your family as you help one another grow. It reaffirms your belief that you are a family of God.

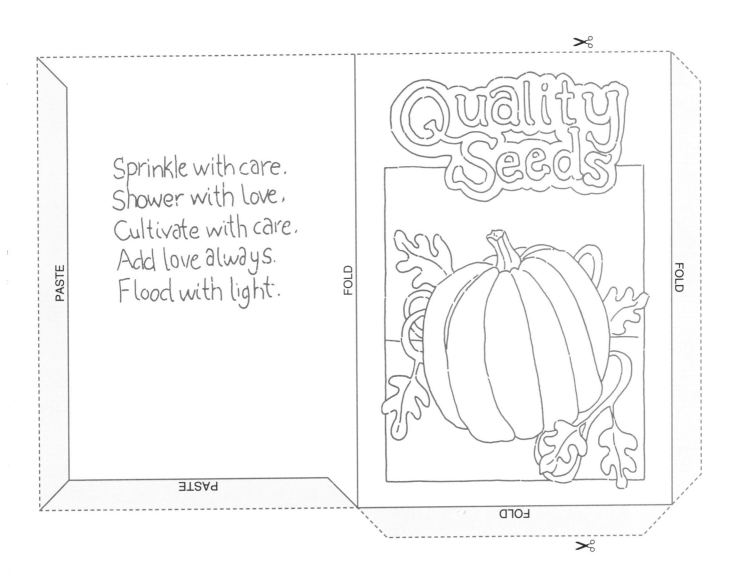

Sprinkle with care.
Shower with love,
Cultivate with care,
Add love always.
Flood with light.

PASTE

PASTE

FOLD

FOLD

FOLD

Quality Seeds

Our Family Pact in a Packet

† **Leader:** We ask God to bless our summertime. We ask God to help us help one another grow.

Leader: Send forth water to make our land rich and our waterways plentiful.

Family: We pray, O God.

Leader: Send forth wind to cool us in the heat.

Family: We pray, O God.

Leader: Let our trees fill with birds and our fields and forests with animals.

Family: We pray, O God.

Leader: Let bread from the fields strengthen us.

Family: We pray, O God.

Leader: Let our faces shine with joy.

Family: We pray, O God.

Leader: *(Pass out slips of paper.)* Let each of us write one way we want to grow this summer.

Leader: May God help us. May God bless and keep us all summer long. May God's face shine on us bright as the sun. May God be gracious to us. May God look kindly on us and bring us peace. Amen.

based on Psalm 103: 10, 13, 15

Make the seed packet on page one. Place your "plans for growing" slips in the packet. Place the packet near your family Bible. After this prayer service, share a special treat.